BRITISH RAILWAYS STEAMING ON THE SOUTHERN REGION

Volume Two

Compiled by
PETER HANDS & COLIN RICHARDS

DEFIANT PUBLICATIONS
190 Yoxall Road, Shirley,
Solihull, West Midlands.

Printed in the United Kingdom by Netherwood Dalton & Co Ltd, Huddersfield, England.

CURRENT STEAM PHOTOGRAPH ALBUMS AVAILABLE
FROM DEFIANT PUBLICATIONS

VOLUME 3
A4 size - Hardback. 100 pages
- 182 b/w photographs.
£7.95 + 75p postage.
ISBN 0 946857 02 4.

VOLUME 4
A4 size - Hardback. 100 pages
- 182 b/w photographs.
£7.95 + 75p postage.
ISBN 0 946857 04 0.

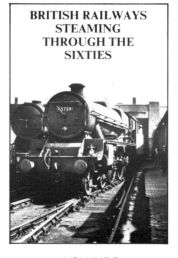

VOLUME 5
A4 size - Hardback. 100 pages
- 180 b/w photographs.
£7.95 + 75p postage.
ISBN 0 946857 06 7.

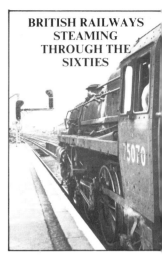

VOLUME 6
A4 size - Hardback. 100 pages
- 182 b/w photographs.
£8.45 + 75p postage.
ISBN 0 946857 08 3.

VOLUME 7
A4 size - Hardback. 100 pages
- 182 b/w photographs.
£8.45 + 75p postage.
ISBN 0 946857 10 5.

VOLUME 8
A4 size - Hardback. 100 pages
- 181 b/w photographs.
£8.95 + 75p postage.
ISBN 0 946857 14 8.

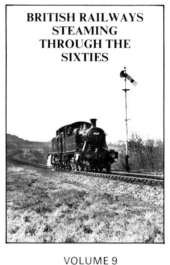

VOLUME 9
A4 size - Hardback. 100 pages
- 182 b/w photographs.
£9.95 + 75p postage.
ISBN 0 946857 18 0.

VOLUME 10
A4 size - Hardback. 100 pages
- 182 b/w photographs.
£9.95 + 75p postage.
ISBN 0 946857 20 2

VOLUME 1
A4 size - Hardback. 100 pages
-180 b/w photographs.
£8.95 + 75p postage.
ISBN 0 946857 12 1.

VOLUME 2
A4 size - Hardback. 100 pages
-180 b/w photographs.
£8.95 + 75p postage.
ISBN 0 946857 13 X.

VOLUME 3
A4 size - Hardback. 100 pages
- 180 b/w photographs.
£9.95 + 75p postage.
ISBN 0 946857 16 4.

VOLUME 4
A4 size - Hardback. 100 pages
- 180 b/w photographs
£9.95 + 75p postage.
ISBN 0 946857 17 2.

BRITISH RAILWAYS
STEAMING
THROUGH THE
FIFTIES

VOLUME 5
IN
PREPARATION
MARCH 1989

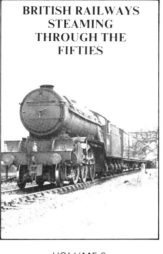

BRITISH RAILWAYS
STEAMING
THROUGH THE
FIFTIES

VOLUME 6
IN
PREPARATION
MARCH 1989

BRITISH RAILWAYS
STEAMING
THROUGH THE
FIFTIES

IN
PREPARATION

VOLUME 7

BRITISH RAILWAYS
STEAMING
THROUGH THE
FIFTIES

IN
PREPARATION

VOLUME 8

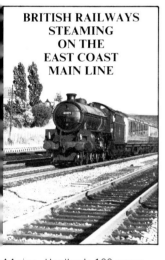

BRITISH RAILWAYS
STEAMING
ON THE
EAST COAST
MAIN LINE

A4 size - Hardback. 100 pages
- 183 b/w photographs.
£8.95 + 75p postage.
ISBN 0 946857 07 5.
(Reprinted July 1988)

BRITISH RAILWAYS
STEAMING ON
THE EX-LNER
LINES

VOLUME 1
A4 size - Hardback. 100 pages
- 187 b/w photographs.
£9.95 + 75p postage.
ISBN 0 946857 19 9.

BRITISH RAILWAYS
STEAMING
ON THE
SOUTHERN REGION

VOLUME 1
A4 size - Hardback. 100 pages
- 188 b/w photographs.
£8.45 + 75p postage.
ISBN 0 946857 09 1.

BRITISH RAILWAYS
STEAMING
ON THE
SOUTHERN REGION

VOLUME 2
A4 size - Hardback. 100 pages
- 181 b/w photographs.
£9.95 + 75p postage.
ISBN 0 946857 21 0

BRITISH RAILWAYS
STEAMING ON THE
WESTERN REGION

VOLUME 1
A4 size - Hardback. 100 pages
- 188 b/w photographs.
£7.95 + 75p postage.
ISBN 0 946857 03 2.

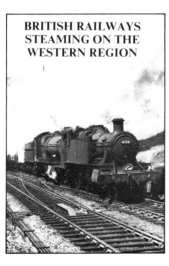

BRITISH RAILWAYS
STEAMING ON THE
WESTERN REGION

VOLUME 2
A4 size - Hardback. 100 pages
- 181 b/w photographs.
£8.45 + 75p postage.
ISBN 0 946857 11 3.

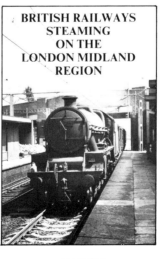

BRITISH RAILWAYS
STEAMING
ON THE
LONDON MIDLAND
REGION

VOLUME 1
A4 size - Hardback. 100 pages
- 184 b/w photographs.
£7.95 + 75p postage.
ISBN 0 946857 05 9.

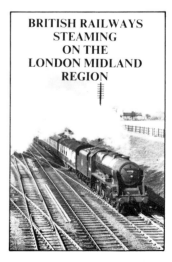

BRITISH RAILWAYS
STEAMING
ON THE
LONDON MIDLAND
REGION

VOLUME 2
A4 size - Hardback. 100 pages
- 181 b/w photographs.
£8.95 + 75p postage.
ISBN 0 946857 15 6.

OTHER TITLES AVAILABLE FROM DEFIANT PUBLICATIONS
PRICES VARY FROM £1 to £3.80 INCLUDING POSTAGE

WHAT HAPPENED TO STEAM

This series of booklets, 50 in all, is designed to inform the reader of the allocations, re-allocations and dates of withdrawal of steam locomotives during their last years of service. From 1957 onwards and finally where the locomotives concerned were stored and subsequently scrapped.

BR STEAM SHED ALLOCATIONS

This series lists all individual steam locomotives based at the different parent depots of B.R. from January 1957 until each depot either closed to steam or closed completely. All regions have been completed with the exception of the London Midland which will be dealt with during 1987.

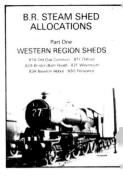

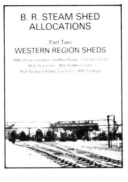
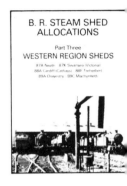

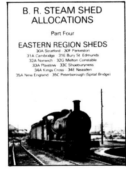
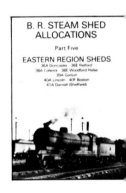

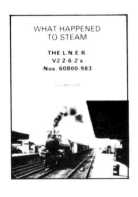

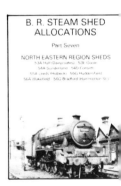

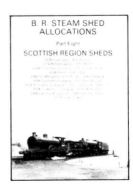

CHASING STEAM ON SHED

PETER HANDS

BARBRYN PRESS £5.95 + 50p POSTAGE

ISBN 0 906160 030

This is an account of a locospotters life during the years of 1956-1968. In 1956 when there were 18,000 or so steam locomotives on B.R. it was every locospotters ambition to set eyes on as many locomotives as possible, especially before they were withdrawn.

Every trainspotter will remember "shed bashing" trips, some official, mostly unofficial, the challenge they represented and the feeling of delight of having achieved of what was regarded in some cases as the impossible. All these are relived with an almost uncanny accurateness.

We also plot through the various exploits of other railway trips of which there are many positively hilarious accounts and these are backed up most commendably by a series of cartoon illustrations which often capture the mood and atmosphere of those days so perfectly.

Depending on your age, this book will either bring back lots of memories, make you realise what you missed or if you were too young to participate will let you realise what good days they were.

....

Lineside Camera Series by G. W. Sharpe.

	8″ + 8″ Approx
BR Standard Steam	36 Pages £2.25 + 30p postage.
Diesels in the Sixties	36 Pages £2.25 + 30p postage.
Named Express	36 Pages £2.25 + 30p postage.
Western Express Steam	36 Pages £2.50 + 30p postage.

ACKNOWLEDGEMENTS

Grateful thanks are extended to the following contributors of photographs not only for their use in this book but for their kind patience and long term loan of negatives/photographs whilst this book was being compiled.

D. ATWELL
FARNHAM

B. W. L. BROOKSBANK
LONDON

R. CARPENTER
BIRMINGHAM

BRIAN COATES
AYLESFORD

A. N. H. GLOVER
BIRMINGHAM

J. HEAD
EASTBOURNE

H. L. HOLLAND
ST. CATHERINES, ONTARIO, CANADA

A. C. INGRAM
WISBECH

R. PICTON
WOLVERHAMPTON

G. W. SHARPE
BARNSLEY

C. STACEY
STONY STRATFORD

D. TITHERIDGE
FAREHAM

T. R. AMOS
TAMWORTH

N. L. BROWNE
ALDERSHOT

J. K. CARTER
MILLHOLME

C. C. DEAMER
SITTINGBOURNE

PETER HAY
HOVE

R. W. HINTON
GLOUCESTER

F. HORNBY
NORTH CHEAM

D. K. JONES
MOUNTAIN ASH

N. E. PREEDY
HUCCLECOTE

JOHN SMITH
LENS OF SUTTON

A. SWAIN
WEMBLEY

MIKE WOOD
BIRMINGHAM

Front Cover - Before the advent of the mass produced motor car, most holiday makers made their way to summer seaside resorts, like Lyme Regis, by train. On an idyllic summer's day in 1960 two Adams 0415 Class 4-4-2 Tanks Nos 30583 and 30582, both from 72A Exmouth Junction are ready to depart from Lyme with a branch train to Axminster. (A. C. Ingram)

ISBN 0 946857 21 0

© P.B. HANDS/C. RICHARDS 1988
FIRST PUBLISHED IN 1988

INTRODUCTION

BRITISH RAILWAYS STEAMING ON THE SOUTHERN REGION - Volume Two, is the second book to concentrate on the Southern Region from the 'British Railways Steaming Through the Sixties' stable.

These books are designed to give the ordinary, everyday steam photographic enthusiast of the 1950's and 1960's a chance to participate in and give pleasure to others whilst recapturing the twilight days of steam.

Apart from the main series, further individual regional albums will be produced from time to time. Wherever possible, no famous names will be found nor will photographs which have been published before be used. Nevertheless, the content and quality of the majority of photographs selected will be second to none.

The layout of BRITISH RAILWAYS STEAMING ON THE SOUTHERN REGION - Volume Two differs from Volume One in as much that it does not concentrate on individual routes. It is almost impossible to repeat the layout of the first book without much duplication, thereby, in the authors opinion, taking away some of the interest.

This second album contains a wide and varied selection of photographs of steam at work and rest from almost one hundred locations on the Southern Region, from as far apart as Cornwall and Kent between 1948 and 1967 when allocated steam finished. Unless otherwise stated, all locomotives are of S.R. origin.

The majority of the photographs used in this album have been contributed by readers of Peter Hands series of booklets entitled "What Happened to Steam" & "BR Steam Shed Allocations" and from readers of the earlier "BR Steaming Through the Sixties" albums. In normal circumstances these may have been hidden from the public eye for ever.

The continuation of the 'BR Steaming' series etc., depends upon you the reader. If you feel you have suitable material of BR steam locomotives between 1948-1968 and wish to contribute them towards this series and other future publications please contact either:

Peter Hands,   Colin Richards,
190 Yoxall Road,   28 Kendrick Close,
Shirley, Solihull,   OR   Damson Parkway, Solihull,
West Midlands B90 3RN.   West Midlands B92 0QD.

CONTENTS

NAMEPLATES - Some example nameplates of S.R. locomotives.

1) H2 Class 4-4-2 No 32424
   Beachy Head. (F. Hornby)

2) 02 Class 0-4-4T No 18
   Ningwood. (A. C. Ingram)

3) Unrebuilt *West Country* Class 4-6-2 No 34020
   Seaton. (Peter Hay)

4) Rebuilt *Battle of Britain* Class 4-6-2 No 34060
   25 Squadron. (D. Titheridge)

5) Rebuilt *Merchant Navy* Class 4-6-2 No 35030
   Elder Dempster Lines. (A. C. Ingram)

6) It is hard to believe that in excess of twenty-one years has now passed by since the sounds of steam echoed in and around the splendid terminus station at Waterloo in the heart of the City of London. The station is all but deserted on a Sunday evening in April 1959 as unrebuilt *Merchant Navy* Class 4-6-2 No 35021 *New Zealand Line* lifts its safety valves prior to departing with the 7.30pm express to Bournemouth. *New Zealand Line*, which had been based at 71B Bournemouth from May 1957 was rebuilt at Eastleigh Works in June 1959. (A. C. Ingram)

7) Sunlight and shadows greet the arrival of unrebuilt *Battle of Britain* Class 4-6-2 No 34070 *Manston* (74C Dover) as it approaches Canterbury East with an up boat train in June 1957. *Manston* was one of six such locomotives which were named after key fighter stations in southern England during the Battle of Britain, the others being *Biggin Hill, Croydon, Hawkinge, Kenley* and *Tangmere*. (Brian Coates)

8) A small group of enthusiasts gather round T9 4-4-0 No 30718 as it replenishes its tender at Yeovil Junction station on 14th August 1960. The occasion is the RCTS 'Greyhound Special' and 30718 was employed on the Salisbury-Yeovil-Weymouth-Wareham-Salisbury legs. Allocated to 72A Exmouth Junction after transfer from 70A Nine Elms in June 1959, 30718 was to end its days at Exmouth in March 1961. (F. Hornby)

9)   Despite being in the early Autumn, bright sunshine blazes down upon this shed scene at Newhaven on 7th October 1962. A gleaming E6 Class 0-6-2-T No 32418 (75A Brighton) poses for the camera after having worked the RCTS 'Sussex Coast' rail-tour along with A1X 'Terrier' Class 0-6-0T No 32636 from Brighton. Behind 32418 is another 'Terrier' 0-6-0T No 32670 which like 32636 was also based at 75A Brighton. (A. Swain)

10) The peace and tranquility of Bere Alston, in the West Country, is disturbed by the plume of steam ascending from the safety valves of unrebuilt *West Country* Class 4-6-2 No 34014 *Budleigh Salterton* (allocation unknown) as it is engaged on shunting duties – circa 1955. Built in November 1945, *Budleigh Salterton* was later rebuilt at Eastleigh in March 1958. Bere Alston still survives today but *Budleigh Salterton* demised in March 1965. (John Smith)

11) During the late 1950's the *Night Ferry* express, from Dover to Victoria was often loaded to 850 tons, the F class sleepers weighing 55 tons each. Double-heading was normal and here we see L1 Class 4-4-0 No 31788 (74C Dover) piloting an unidentified unrebuilt *Battle of Britain* Class 4-6-2 down Grosvenor bank into Victoria on 31st May 1957. (Peter Hay)

12) At one time the London & South Western Railway indicated engine classes by the running number of one of the engines in the class. 0-6-0 No 30306, photographed in the shed yard at 71A Eastleigh, in April 1952, was a member of the 700 Class, popularly known by enginemen as 'Black Motors'. Re-boilering of the original Drummond design by R. W. Urie gave them a long and useful life, in the case of 30306, until April 1962. (Peter Hay)

13) With the winter all but over, on 30th March 1957, a superbly maintained *Schools* Class 4-4-0 No 30934 *St. Lawrence* (73B Bricklayers Arms) lays a trail of sulphur as it steams through Sevenoaks with the 11.10am Hastings to Charing Cross express. Built at Eastleigh in 1935, *St. Lawrence* was equipped with a multiple jet blastpipe and large diameter chimney. (F. Hornby)

14) Before 1923, St. Leonards on the Sussex Coast was the boundary between the SECR and the LBSCR. The latter's depot at West Marina housed engines from both companies, as well as the famous SR *Schools* Class 4-4-0's. Standing in the shed yard on 25th May 1957 is H Class 0-4-4T No 31269, behind which is Brighton 'Terrier' A1X Class 0-6-0T No 32678 both of which were resident to the then coded 74E depot. It lost its 'parent' status in June 1958. (Peter Hay)

15) An extremely clean H16 Class 4-6-2T No 30517 simmers gently outside its home shed at 70B Feltham on 4th October 1952. Pure freight engines were a rarity on the Southern and this class only consisted of five locomotives. Designed by Urie, they were introduced in 1921 with a power classification of 6F and a tractive effort of 28,200 lbs. All five examples of the class were withdrawn in November 1962, from Feltham. (A. N. H. Glover)

16) An overcast and murky day at Basingstoke on 15th October 1963. To the left of the picture, passing through the station, light engine, is an unidentified rebuilt *West Country/Battle of Britain* Class 4-6-2. Facing the camera is *Merchant Navy* Class 4-6-2 No 35019 *French Line CGT*, from 70A Nine Elms and rebuilt in May 1959, along with BR Class 5 4-6-0 No 73116 *Iseult*, also from Nine Elms. Both engines are on passenger duties. (J. K. Carter)

17) Blazing sunshine, associated with high summer, beats down on Exeter (Central) on 12th July 1957. Standing light engine in the station is an unrebuilt *Merchant Navy* Class 4-6-2 No 35004 *Cunard White Star*, from 72B Salisbury. Constructed in October 1941, at the height of the Second World War, *Cunard White Star* was later rebuilt at Eastleigh in June 1958. (F. Hornby)

18) In stark contrast to the above picture is this photograph taken on a cold and dreary day in December 1963. A filthy W Class 2-6-4T No 31913 leaks steam as it struggles for adhesion whilst passing its home shed at 75C Norwood Junction with a lengthy Bricklayers Arms to Waddon coal train. During this same month, 31913 was transferred to its final base at 70B Feltham from whence it was condemned in March 1964. (A. C. Ingram)

19) 02 Class 0-4-4T No 14 *Fishbourne* looks in fine fettle, but has lost its nameplates as it runs round the train it has brought in from Ryde after arrival at Ventnor on an unknown date in 1963. During the 1950's and 1960's the Isle of Wight rail network was decimated and the only stretch of line still operated by British Rail in 1988 runs from Ryde (Pier) to Shanklin. Ventnor was closed in 1966. (D. Atwell)

20) Despite steam being on the run in the south east of England in June 1960, the *Golden Arrow* was still entrusted to the capable hands of the old order of traction, as it would be for a further twelve months. The down express is being hauled by unrebuilt *West Country* Class 4-6-2 No 34091 *Weymouth* (73A Stewarts Lane), which is swathed in smoke and steam as it bursts from under a road bridge at speed near to Marden between Paddock Wood and Ashford. (Brian Coates)

21)	70A Nine Elms was the last haven for the L1 Class 4-4-0's. Made redundant from the Kent Coast lines by electrification in June 1959, all fifteen members of the class were sent to Nine Elms. From August 1959 their numbers were gradually whittled down until, by the end of 1961 there was only one example left in service, No 31786. This particular engine is photographed in the yard at Nine Elms on 27th February 1960, two years before withdrawal. (R. Picton)

22)	A highly polished H2 Class 4-4-2 No 32421 *South Foreland* (75A Brighton) is the subject of admiration at Guildford on 6th February 1955. *South Foreland* was at the end of its journey having been in charge of the RCTS 'Hampshireman' special from Waterloo via Staines. The last 'Atlantic' in service was 32424 *Beachy Head*, withdrawn on 13th April 1958. (F. Hornby)

23)	During the sixties, the vast majority of trains to and from Weymouth were still steam hauled. BR Class 5 4-6-0 No 73080 *Merlin*, from the nearby home shed, coded 70G, is bathed in brilliant sunshine as it rattles its passenger train past Weymouth marshalling yards in June 1966. The name, *Merlin*, was once carried by *King Arthur* Class 4-6-0 No 30740. (G. W. Sharpe)

24)	G6 Class 0-6-0T No 30162 (depot unknown) simmers and gurgles in the sunshine at 72A Exmouth Junction in April 1956. This class of engines were designed by Adams and introduced into service in 1894. By January 1957 there were only ten survivors, scattered all over the Southern system. 30162 was still in service, based at 72D Plymouth (Friary) being withdrawn from there in March 1958. (G. W. Sharpe)

25)   A close-up of the front end of rebuilt *West Country* Class 4-6-2 No 34025 *Whimple*, a visitor to 70F Bournemouth from
      70D Eastleigh as it rests against the buffer stops in the shed yard on 13th August 1965. During the mid-sixties steam was
      on the decline on the Southern with falling standards of cleanliness and maintenance and towards the end most steam
      locomotives were devoid of name and numberplates etc. *Whimple*, built in March 1946 was rebuilt in October 1957 and
      by October 1965 was allocated to Bournemouth, where it was destined to die in July 1967. (A. C. Ingram)

26) From the onset of the railways coming into being at Clapham Junction, legions of tank locomotives were utilised to ferry passenger stock to and from Waterloo. In the latter years of steam on the Southern, the older SR classes were phased out and their duties taken over by BR standard locomotives. A surprisingly clean BR Class 4 2-6-4T No 80143 (70A Nine Elms) is on ECS duty at Clapham on 13th August 1964. (H. L. Holland)

27) Hazy sunshine filters through the high cloud base as unrebuilt *Battle of Britain* Class 4-6-2 No 34068 *Kenley* (73A Stewarts Lane) approaches Maidstone with a holiday extra to the coast in August 1960. Made surplus to requirements in this area of the Southern in May 1961, *Kenley* was transferred to 72B Salisbury. It was taken out of revenue earning service from Salisbury in December 1963 and scrapped at Eastleigh three months later. (Brian Coates)

28) The single line branch between Eridge and Hailsham in Sussex closed in 1965 and the people of Horam then had to rely on buses as their only means of travel by public transport. On 1st June 1957 the 3.39pm from Tunbridge Wells to Eastbourne arrives at Horam with its old two coach push and pull set, with modern motive power in the shape of BR Class 4 2-6-4T No 80154 (75A Brighton), which was virtually brand new. (Peter Hay)

29) Dazzling sunshine reflects off the smart exterior of 0298 Class 2-4-0WT No 30585, seen at rest in the yard of its home shed at 72F Wadebridge on 29th June 1960. Along with sister engines Nos 30586 and 30587, these were the only three survivors of a once numerous class of Well tanks. They were employed on the china clay lines to Ruthern Bridge and Wenford Bridge and all three survived until December 1962. Nos 30585 and 30587 are preserved. (N. E. Preedy)

30) A line-up of motive power on the yard at 74A Ashford on a grey 17th May 1958. On view are BR Class 2 2-6-2T No 84020 and Z Class 0-8-0T No 30951, both of which were Ashford based engines. 84020 moved on to 73A Stewarts Lane in January 1961, eventually ending its days at 6G Llandudno Junction in October 1964. 30951 was transferred away to 72A Exmouth Junction in May 1959 being withdrawn from there in November 1962. (F. Hornby)

31) The bitter cold of a winter's day helps to highlight the exhaust from U Class 2-6-0 No 31798 as it speeds through Earlsfield between Clapham Junction and Wimbledon with a down empty stock train bound for Southampton Docks on 16th February 1957. 31798, allocated to 70C Guildford, moved on to pastures new at 72C Yeovil in February 1960 and remained alive there until condemnation in September 1964. (N. L. Browne)

32) Standing astride a maze of third rail tracks, H16 Class 4-6-2T No 30519 (70B Feltham) waits patiently at Clapham Junction with the empty stock of the *Bournemouth Belle* on 10th September 1960. For a period of time between February 1960 and May 1961, all five members of the class, had spells of duty based at 71A Eastleigh for use on the Fawley branch. 30519 was based there from February 1961 but returned to Feltham the following month. (N. L. Browne)

33) A spotter relaxes on the platform at Basingstoke as members of the staff discuss an unknown subject on 22nd August 1959. The latter trio of railwaymen ignore the passing of rebuilt *West Country* Class 4-6-2 No 34047 *Callington* (71B Bournemouth) as it sweeps by with a down Waterloo to West of England express. Built in November 1946, *Callington* was rebuilt in November 1958 and was condemned from Bournemouth in June 1967. (F. Hornby)

34) Multiple pipework along the footplate framing of H Class 0-4-4T No 31164 indicates that the engine is 'motor fitted' to work push and pull trains. As this scene is at Tonbridge in April 1952, the Hawkhurst or Westerham branches seem the most likely place of this employment. 31164 was withdrawn from 73J Tonbridge in October 1959 and cut up at Ashford the same month. (Peter Hay)

35) The photographer is scrutinised by a passer-by who has trespassed into the viewfinder as the shutter clicked at Okehampton on 28th June 1960. The original subject matter of the man with the camera, unrebuilt *Battle of Britain* Class 4-6-2 No 34072 *257 Squadron*, from 72A Exmouth Junction, steams and sizzles impatiently whilst awaiting its next turn of duty. (N. L. Browne)

36) Back to back terraced houses, most of which probably housed railwaymen and their families dominate the background of this picture of the shed yard at 75C Norwood Junction on 9th June 1962. In the foreground is one of Norwood Junction's resident W Class 2-6-4 Tanks No 31918. In the left background is U1 Class 2-6-0 No 31900, another locomotive which was a native of Norwood Junction. (D. K. Jones)

37) Although this appears to be a goods working, the train behind 'Greyhound' T9 Class 4-4-0 No 30718 (70A Nine Elms) is a passenger service, with a fitted cattle wagon as the leading vehicle. As usual, the arrival from the Guildford line in November 1957, has been stopped at Redhill 'B' signalbox home signals because of congestion in the station. (Peter Hay)

38) One can almost hear the unique sounds that only a Bulleid Pacific can make as rebuilt *West Country* Class 4-6-2 No 34042 *Dorchester* steams away from the lengthy down platform at Bournemouth (Central) in June 1963. At this stage in time *Dorchester*, constructed in October 1946 and rebuilt in January 1959, was a 70F Bournemouth based engine. It moved on to 70D Eastleigh in September 1964. (G. W. Sharpe)

39) The unkempt shed building at 75F Tunbridge Wells is having repair work done to it on 1st September 1955. A young fireman takes it easy as his charge, Drummond motor fitted M7 Class 0-4-4T No 30056, built at Nine Elms in January 1906, has steam to spare as it waits to take charge of an East Grinstead motor train. 30056 had a further eight years of service ahead before being withdrawn from 70F Bournemouth in December 1963. (F. Hornby)

40) Without the thoughtfully placed destination plaques beneath the bridge at Folkestone Junction this could easily fall into the 'C.B.A.' or 'Could Be Anywhere' category prints, an opinion once voiced by one of the contributors. Unrebuilt *Battle of Britain* Class 4-6-2 No 34081 *92 Squadron* passes the camera with a Dover to Victoria express on 3rd August 1952. (R. W. Hinton)

41) *King Arthur* Class 4-6-0 No 30765 *Sir Gareth* (70D Basingstoke) emerges from beneath the giant coaling plant at 70A Nine Elms on 25th February 1961. A closer examination will reveal that much of its fresh coal supply consists of slack which will no doubt displease the next rostered fireman. *Sir Gareth* was destined to be one of the last surviving *King Arthur's* being condemned from Basingstoke shed in September 1962. (N. L. Browne)

2) A freshly withdrawn W Class 2-6-4T No 31925, late of 75C Norwood Junction, lies forlorn and derelict, awaiting its fate with a condemned unrebuilt *Battle of Britain* Class 4-6-2 (identity not known) in the shed yard at 70D Eastleigh on 10th November 1963. To the right of 31925 is the coaling stage road, all but empty apart from a BR type locomotive. (N. L. Browne)

3) The ballast at Pevensey between Bexhill and Lewes, looks clean enough in June 1959, but nevertheless the weed killing train is in action to make sure it stays that way. K Class 2-6-0 No 32347, a 75E Three Bridges engine, is in charge. All seventeen members of the class were condemned in November and December 1962. 32347 found itself grounded at 75D Stewarts Lane after withdrawal being scrapped on site nine months later. (Peter Hay)

44)   With its speed well into the eighties, unrebuilt *Merchant Navy* Class 4-6-2 No 35001 *Channel Packet*, allocated to 73A
       Stewarts Lane, roars past a rake of cattle trucks and passes Ashford with an up boat train bound for London in April
       1959. The construction of the *Merchant Navy* Class locomotives took some eight years from start to finish with *Channel*
       Packet being the pioneer engine in February 1941. It was also one of the first to be withdrawn, in November 1964. Final
       disposal came in May 1965 at Birds, Morriston, Swansea. (Brian Coates)

26

45) Only in high summer was it light enough for the 6.10pm from Tonbridge to Brighton to be photographed at London Road, almost at the end of its journey, as seen here in June 1957. D1 Class 4-4-0 No 31492 (74D Tonbridge) will be turned and serviced at 75A Brighton shed and will take the last train of the evening back home to Tonbridge, after darkness has curtailed photography for the day. (Peter Hay)

46) Another photograph of 'Greyhound' T9 Class 4-4-0 No 30718 on special duty, as previously mentioned on page 7. This time, 30718 is photographed at Salisbury prior to leaving for Weymouth via Yeovil Junction on 14th August 1960. After withdrawal in March 1961 it is doubtful if it would have been in the highly polished condition as seen on this special. 30718 was put to the torch at Eastleigh in April 1961. (Peter Hay)

47) After sixty years of archaic passenger services as part of the ancient Bodmin & Wadebridge Railway, Bodmin got a proper station, by courtesy of the LSWR in 1895. British Railways called it Bodmin (North) and on 17th August 1959 the 5.48pm to Wadebridge and Padstow was waiting to leave behind 02 Class 30236 (72F Wadebridge). Today, trains get no closer than Bodmin Road on the Western Region main line. (Peter Hay)

48) The shed yard at 71B Bournemouth as photographed from the station car park end in July 1962. In the left of the picture is M7 Class 0-4-4T No 30057, to the right of which is unrebuilt *West Country* Class 4-6-2 No 34041 *Wilton*, both of which were local engines. On the extreme right is a visitor from 71A Eastleigh – U Class 2-6-0 No 31639. In the background, behind 30057 is the elevated signalbox situated above the down platform. (G. W. Sharpe)

9) In ex. works condition, a locally based rebuilt *West Country* Class 4-6-2 No 34012 *Launceston* awaits its next rostered working in the depot yard at 75A Brighton on 7th October 1962. Behind the tender of *Launceston*, the cavernous roof of the station can just be discerned. Built in October 1945, *Launceston* was converted into its final condition in January 1958. (B. W. L. Brooksbank)

) With a dark sky providing a backcloth, a Bricklayers Arms to Dover van train, approaches Selling, between Faversham and Canterbury in April 1956 behind a 74C Dover based *King Arthur* Class 4-6-0 No 30798 *Sir Hectimere*. An early victim of third rail electrification, *Sir Hectimere* was drafted to 72B Salisbury, where it spent its last days until withdrawn in June 1962. (Brian Coates)

51) A far from clean rebuilt *West Country* Class 4-6-2 No 34040 *Crewkerne* has been coaled and watered and is blowing off impatiently next to the shed building at 70G Weymouth in August 1964. Built in September 1946, rebuilding of *Crewkerne* took place some fourteen years later. This locomotive was a particular favourite of Bournemouth shed and was condemned from there, after many years of service, in July 1967. (G. W. Sharpe)

52) Like Bere Alston, Bodmin (North), Okehampton and Wadebridge, Ilfracombe was also an outpost for Southern Region steam. The penultimate Light Pacific – unrebuilt *Battle of Britain* Class 4-6-2 No 34109 *Sir Trafford Leigh-Mallory* (72A Exmouth Junction) is preparing to attach itself to the empty stock of a passenger train in the sidings which were adjacent to the platforms on 2nd July 1960. Ilfracombe station closed completely in 1970. (N. L. Browne)

53) South London electric services didn't come to a total halt just because the Queen was going to the Derby and one has just passed the Royal Train as it departs from Victoria on 7th June 1957. Her Majesty is in the second Pullman and a gleaming *Schools* Class 4-4-0 No 30939 *Leatherhead* (73B Bricklayers Arms), complete with a multiple jet blastpipe and double chimney has been given a special finish for this important duty. (Peter Hay)

54) A trio of smoke-blackened C Class 0-6-0's are lined up outside their home shed of 73B Bricklayers Arms in September 1956. Only the front one can be identified – No 31280 which was to remain at Bricklayers Arms until transferred to 74D Tonbridge in March 1957. Withdrawn from normal service in June 1962, 31280 was allocated to Service Stock at Ashford Works until final condemnation in July 1963. (G. W. Sharpe)

55) The spacious layout at Faversham can clearly be seen in this photograph which was taken on 21st March 1959. There are sidings, complete with intricate pointwork, various semaphore signals, guards vans, third rails and just visible in the right of the picture is a signalbox. A begrimed unrebuilt *Battle of Britain* Class 4-6-2 No 34068 *Kenley* (73A Stewarts Lane) comes into the station with an up express. (N. L. Browne)

56) Quite a large number of LMS Tank locomotives were allocated to sheds in many areas of the Southern Region. Amongst these were examples of the Ivatt LMS Class 3 2-6-2T's, two of which are noted, running bunker-first, through Eastleigh station with a train of mineral empties on 1st August 1962. The nearest one can be identified as 41323, a long way from its home base at 72A Exmouth Junction. (N. L. Browne)

57) With steam to spare a 70A Nine Elms L1 Class 4-4-0 No 31786 is employed on a breakdown train at Gloucester Road Junction, Selhurst on 18th June 1961. In the background a more modern structure has been added on to the older section of a once well known typewriter firm. The amateurish way in which the firm was advertised, mostly in white-wash lettering, would hardly have enhanced the reputation of the company. (B. W. L. Brooksbank)

58) In May 1956, the approach to Brighton station was still dominated by the bulk of the locomotive works on the right. As 'The Fast' (non-stop to Victoria) makes its hourly timetabled departure on the left, D1 Class 4-4-0 No 31470 (74D Tonbridge) rattles over pointwork as it brings in a light-weight service from Tonbridge. (Peter Hay)

59) One of the resident S15 Class 4-6-0's No 30832 is ready for the road at 72B Salisbury on 2nd June 1951. As it was still allocated there in January 1957 it is only fair to assume that it was also based there during the intervening years. It was to remain at Salisbury until condemned in January 1964. Behind 30832 is unrebuilt *West Country* Class 4-6-2 No 34013 *Okehampton*, rebuilt in October 1957. (A. N. H. Glover)

60) Equipped with the original small chimney, *Schools* Class 4-4-0 No 30922 *Marlborough*, newly transferred to 73A Stewarts Lane from 73G Ramsgate, darkens the sky as it climbs out of Maidstone with an up boat train in July 1959. *Marlborough* remained at Stewarts Lane until November 1961, when it went to 75A Brighton being withdrawn the same month. (Brian Coates)

61) An early morning train to Tonbridge passes 75B Redhill shed in August 1957 with L1 Class 4-4-0 No 31777, a 75A Brighton engine, in charge. Just visible to the left of the 'B' signalbox home signals are a Q Class 0-6-0 and a GWR 4300 Class 2-6-0 which has arrived from Reading. 31777 survived in service until withdrawn from 70A Nine Elms in September 1959. (Peter Hay)

62) Andover shed (S.R.) on 14th May 1955. This small depot was hosting a visiting 70A Nine Elms U Class 2-6-0 No 31634 which is seen in very acceptable external condition. Built at Brighton Works in 1931, 31634 was fitted with outside steam pipes. It remained at Nine Elms in revenue earning service until no longer required in December 1963. (F. Hornby)

63)   BR Class 4 4-6-0 No 75067, from 75D Stewarts Lane, minus shedplate, accelerates out of Brighton in a flurry of steam
and smoke and heads for Preston Park with the empty stock of a sleeping car train, in July 1963. The last fifteen members
of this class, Nos 75065-75079 were allocated to depots on the Southern Region. All were equipped with double
chimney's and because there were no water trough facilities on the Southern, they were paired with larger capacity
tenders. Three locomotives from this particular batch are either in a state of working preservation or in stages of
restoration, these being Nos 75069/78/79. (A. C. Ingram)

36

64) Many of the ex. London, Brighton & South Coast Railway, Billington designed E4 Class 0-6-2 Tanks, survived well into British Railways days. Some twelve years or so have passed since nationalisation came about, when No 32500 (70A Nine Elms) was captured by the camera, reversing light engine into Waterloo station to take up a down empty stock duty in May 1960. The last survivor of the class, No 32479 (75A Brighton) was condemned in June 1963. (A. C. Ingram)

65) A work-stained 02 Class 0-4-4T No 28 *Ashey* (70G Ryde) drifts into Ryde St. John's Road station from Ryde Pier with a rake of ancient stock, which was the hallmark of services in steam days on the Isle of Wight, on 19th September 1964. Steam has long since gone on services on the island but at least the station is still alive, albeit with ex. London underground transport, complete with the associated third rail system. (R. Picton)

66) On Whit Sunday in 1956, the 11.08am Redhill to Brighton, via Tonbridge, was carrying the reporting number 142 as well as the usual headcode, no doubt to help the busy signalman at Tonbridge to send it in the right direction. L1 Class 4-4-0 No 31785, from 73D Gillingham, heads a three coach 'birdcage' set past Falmer, just a few short miles from the end of the journey. (Peter Hay)

67) Another far-flung outpost for Southern steam was at Padstow, in Cornwall, a seaside resort on the Atlantic Coast. Although situated many, many miles from Waterloo, a portion of the once famous *Atlantic Coast Express* used to find its way here. The station closed to passengers in 1967. In September 1960, our old friend 'Greyhound' T9 Class 4-4-0 No 30718 (72A Exmouth Junction) was to be found on the turntable. (A. C. Ingram)

68) The end of the line has been reached for three *Schools* Class 4-4-0's Nos 30914 *Eastbourne*, 30904 *Lancing* and 30938 *St. Olave's* as they wait, minus nameplates, for the cutter's torch at Ashford Works on 21st August 1961. All had been withdrawn the previous month from 75B Redhill, 70D Basingstoke and 70A Nine Elms respectively. Within a further month or so, all would have been reduced to small piles of scrap metal. (D. K. Jones)

69) One of the Southern branch lines which was never affected by modernisation, right up until total closure was the line from Havant to Hayling Island. Running round its train at Havant on 25th October 1962 is 'Terrier' A1X Class 0-6-0T No 32678, from 71A Eastleigh. The line and its associated stations at Hayling Island, Langston and North Hayling, fell victims to the Beeching axe in 1963. (N. L. Browne)

70) The peaceful surroundings at Waddon, between Norwood Junction and Sutton, are disturbed momentarily by the rattle of a Norwood to Epsom loose-coupled freight train which is being hauled by U Class 2-6-0 No 31616, a 75C Norwood Junction engine, in July 1963. In comparison with other regions, freight traffic on the Southern was very sparce indeed. (A. C. Ingram)

71) More Southern Region steam in the West Country, this time at Barnstaple Junction, the pivot of lines once leading to Halwill Junction, Ilfracombe, Lynton and Taunton, all long since closed. Today, the only line still open from Barnstaple, goes to Exeter. A Southern owned 'userper', ex. LMS Ivatt Class 2 2-6-2T No 41295, based at the close at hand shed, coded 72E, poses for the camera, in the station on 29th September 1960. (N. L. Browne)

72) Many services on the Redhill to Reading line were hauled by locomotives of former Great Western origin. Employed on such a service in June 1963, is ex. GWR *Manor* Class 4-6-0 No 7813 *Freshford Manor* (81D Reading), near to North Camp, between Guildford and Farnborough. *Freshford Manor* has just passed under the bridge carrying the Woking to Alton line, part of which can be seen to the right of the picture. (N. L. Browne)

73) The disadvantage of winter photography, without the aid of flash, were the short hours of daylight which were available. There is just enough bright sunshine left to highlight the passing of the down *Golden Arrow*, from Dover to Waterloo, on 2nd January 1960, photographed near to Tonbridge with unrebuilt *Battle of Britain* Class 4-6-2 No 34086 *219 Squadron*, from 73A Stewarts Lane, in charge. (D. K. Jones)

74) There are no prizes for guessing that this is an 'Open Day' at Eastleigh Works on 1st August 1962. A St. Trinian's style mob of schoolchildren swarm like locusts over B4 Class 0-4-0T No 30096 (71A Eastleigh), which is ex. works. One of the taller lads is peering into the funnel – was it out of curiosity or had he stuffed his horrid little sister down it!! (N. L. Browne)

75) GWR and SR coaches alternated on the Birkenhead-Hastings through service in the 1950's and on this August afternoon in 1954, the products of Swindon are coasting through the South Downs. 75A Brighton shed has provided Brighton 'Atlantic' H2 Class 4-4-2 No 32425 *Trevose Head* to work the Redhill-Brighton part of the journey, seen here about three miles away from Brighton. (Peter Hay)

76)   *Schools* Class 4-4-0 No 30902 *Wellington*, from 74E St. Leonards, prepares to depart from Waterloo (Eastern Section) on 30th March 1957, with the 2.25pm Charing Cross to Hastings passenger. Built at Eastleigh Works in 1930, *Wellington* was to remain in service until December 1962, being withdrawn from 70A Nine Elms, after thirty-two years of sterling work. (F. Hornby)

77)   72B Salisbury hosts a visiting 72A Exmouth Junction unrebuilt *West Country* Class 4-6-2 No 34016 *Bodmin* on a July day in 1957. Constructed in November 1945, *Bodmin* had its air-smoothed casing removed whilst being rebuilt in March 1958. Withdrawn from 70D Eastleigh in June 1964, *Bodmin* was stored there for six months or so before being despatched to Barry Docks where it lay rotting until the Mid-Hants Railway saved it in July 1972. (G. W. Sharpe)

78)	Although the multiple jet blastpipes and large diameter chimney's may well have enhanced the performance of the twenty members of the *Schools* Class 4-4-0's to which they were applied, they did nothing for their looks. One of these examples, a begrimed No 30920 *Rugby*, from 74B Ramsgate, threads its way through Ashford with an express working in March 1957. (G. W. Sharpe)

79)	The Southern, in B.R. days had a number of 0-6-0's on its books, classified as – 700, Q, 0395, C, 01, C2X and Q1's. The 700 Class consisted of thirty locomotives and one of their number, 30346 was captured by the camera by the coaling plant in the yard of its home shed at 70B Feltham on 9th February 1957. The final examples still in service were all withdrawn in December 1962. (N. L. Browne)

80) BR Class 5 4-6-0 No 73117, a visitor from 70A Nine Elms, dominates this picture, taken in the shed yard at 75A Brighton on 12th January 1957. All of the series of BR Class 5's Nos 73080-73089 and 73110-73119 were later to carry names once allocated to some of the *King Arthur* Class 4-6-0's which had been withdrawn. In the case of 73117 it was named *Vivien* from 30748. (F. Hornby)

81) The S15 Class 4-6-0's were derived from the ideas of two designers, the first batch by Urie Nos 30496-30515 and the latter ones by Maunsell Nos 30823-30847. One of the Maunsell locomotives No 30823, from 72B Salisbury, starts a freight out of Yeovil in October 1962. Withdrawals of the Maunsell engines did not commence until November 1962, when 30826 was condemned. The class was rendered extinct in normal service in September 1965. (G. W. Sharpe)

82) A close-up of 02 Class 0-4-4T No 17 *Seaview* taken inside the shed at 70H Ryde on 10th August 1966, a few short months before steam was to disappear from the Isle of Wight. At this date in time there were still eleven examples of these engines at work, these being Nos 14 *Fishbourne*, 16 *Ventnor*, 17 *Seaview*, 20 *Shanklin*, 22 *Brading*, 24 *Calbourne*, 27 *Merstone*, 28 *Ashey*, 31 *Chale*, 33 *Bembridge* and 35 *Freshwater*. No 24 *Calbourne*, withdrawn in March 1967 is preserved in active service at Havenstreet. (C. C. Deamer)

46

83) A plume of black smoke erupts from the chimney of BR *Britannia* Class 4-6-2 No 70004 *William Shakespeare*, the pride of 73A Stewarts Lane, as it bursts from beneath a road bridge near Marden, at speed, with the down *Golden Arrow* in June 1954. Who would have guessed that in later years *William Shakespeare* would end up being allocated to depots like Carlisle (Canal) and Stockport. (Brian Coates)

84) 1988 is the 400th anniversary of Sir Francis Drake's magnificent defeat of the Spanish Armada. His namesake, *Lord Nelson* Class 4-6-0 No 30851, from 71A Eastleigh, leans to a curve whilst departing from Southampton (Central) with a down Waterloo to Bournemouth express on 18th April 1961. Condemned eight months later, this *Sir Francis Drake* had an ignominious end by courtesy of the cutter's torch at Eastleigh in May 1962. (T. R. Amos)

85) Going by the date, 30th August 1958, this is probably one of the August Bank Holiday days. Carrying a 'special' disc and train reporting/destination codes, BR Class 4 4-6-0 No 75069, based at 74C Dover, passes through Bromley South, between Shortlands and Bickley and heads for the coast with a Victoria-Ramsgate passenger train. It is no doubt packed with excited trippers looking forward to some sea, sunshine and sand. (N. L. Browne)

86) The K Class 2-6-0's were probably unique with regards to their looks, compared to other classes of locomotives. Designed by Billington, they were built at Brighton, being first introduced into service in 1913, eventually totalling seventeen in number. No 32349, built in 1920, poses for the camera outside the roundhouse of its home shed of 70F Fratton on 6th October 1956. (F. Hornby)

87) A view taken in and around the straight shed at 74D Tonbridge on 11th May 1957. Simmering in front of the depot are H Class 0-4-4T No 31310, a 'foreigner' from 75F Tunbridge Wells and a home-based C Class 0-6-0 No 31590. To the left of 31310, the smokebox numberplate of Q1 Class 0-6-0 No 33033, another Tonbridge engine, can just be made out. (N. L. Browne)

88) East Putney, between Wandsworth Town and Wimbledon Park, owned by London Transport, hosts the unusual combination of M7 Class 0-4-0T No 30243 (70A Nine Elms), as it pilots an unidentified *Battle of Britain* Class 4-6-2 through the station with milk empties from Clapham Junction to Salisbury and the West of England – circa 1956. The former LSWR station at East Putney had closed as early as 1941. (John Smith)

89) Weymouth, once the property of the G.W.R. was handed over to the Southern Region in February 1958. The Southern influence at the local shed, coded 71G, was not noticed for a long time with the allocation keeping its ex. GWR locomotives. In later years the allocation was supplanted by various SR, LMS and BR types. Rebuilt *Battle of Britain* Class 4-6-2 No 34077 *603 Squadron* (70A Nine Elms) drifts by the camera on 26th August 1964. (Mike Wood)

90) The main influence at Reading was provided by the GWR with its fine station at Reading (General). There was also a smaller Southern station, Reading (South) which closed in 1965. There was a small sub-shed provided for the latter station's needs and on 9th September 1962, a 70C Guildford U Class 2-6-0 No 31797 was captured by the camera, in steam in the yard. (N. E. Preedy)

91) A virtually brand new BR Class 5 4-6-0 No 73082, later named *Camelot* after the withdrawn *King Arthur* Class 4-6-0 No 30742, stands in an apparently deserted yard at its home depot of 73A Stewarts Lane in September 1955. 73082 moved on to 70A Nine Elms in May 1959 where it remained until transferred to 70C Guildford, its final home, in May 1965, being withdrawn from there in June 1966. (G. W. Sharpe)

92) The elderly load behind M7 Class 0-4-4T No 30053 (allocation unknown) is just 43 ½ tons, and as it is going downhill at this point the smoke effect seems hardly justified. In October 1953 this Brighton to Horsham train has just left the Coastway West at Shoreham Junction and is heading for its next stop at Bramber, which was destined to close during 1966. (Peter Hay)

93) The H15 Class 4-6-0's were first introduced in 1914 and were ungainly looking locomotives, with a power classification of 4P5F. No 30335, from 72B Salisbury, rattles an up stone train past Basingstoke shed in March 1959. 30335 was first built by Drummond and later rebuilt by Urie and Maunsell. It was taken out of service from Salisbury in June 1959. (Brian Coates)

94) A gnarled and mis-shaped tree looks down upon the railway scene at Callington, in the West of England in April 1961. One of the few surviving 02 Class 0-4-4 Tanks still in service on the mainland, No 30193, from 83H Plymouth (Friary), is photographed light engine, between shunting duties. Callington, once owned by the Plymouth, Devonport and South Western Junction Railway, closed completely in 1966. (G. W. Sharpe)

95) Fourteen of the 'Greyhound' T9 Class 4-4-0's were still in service during 1960. One of their number, a smoke-blackened 72A Exmouth Junction based No 30715 is ready for its next duty at Okehampton on 28th June 1960. There was a further year of service still in front of 30715 before it succumbed to condemnation from Exmouth Junction in July 1961. (N. L. Browne)

96) A mid-morning Victoria to Ramsgate express tops the bank out of Herne Bay, in February 1958 with unrebuilt *West Country* Class 4-6-2 No 34101 *Hartland*, from 73A Stewarts Lane in charge. *Hartland*, built by British Railways in January 1950, was rebuilt ten years later, in September 1960. It was withdrawn from 70D Eastleigh in July 1966 and after some twelve years in store at Barry is now preserved on the Peak Forest Railway. (Brian Coates)

97) An immaculate N Class 2-6-0 No 31862, a visitor from 75B Redhill, is turned on the exposed table at the far end of 74C Dover shed in July 1954. These Maunsell designed engines, of 4P5F motive power classification, were 'maids of all work' and were often pressed into service on heavy passenger trains, especially during the summer months when there was usually a shortage of more powerful locomotives. (G. W. Sharpe)

98) Only desperate crews used the water column at the west end of Lewes station, for Brighton and the end of their journey was only a few miles away. In November 1956 there were no problems for D1 Class 4-4-0 No 31470 as it called in with a local train from Tonbridge. The end was also in sight for the revenue earning days of 31470, being withdrawn from 73J Tonbridge in June 1959. (Peter Hay)

99) A filthy dirty unrebuilt *Merchant Navy* Class 4-6-2 No 35001 *Channel Packet* (72A Exmouth Junction) pollutes the clean Devon atmosphere at Axminster on 2nd July 1953. *Channel Packet*, equipped with short smoke deflectors, was in charge of a down Waterloo to Exeter (Central) express. Note the pre-cast concrete sections of station fencing which were a common sight on the Southern Region. (F. Hornby)

100) By 5th March 1960, 73B Bricklayers Arms was in the stages of being run down, prior to total closure in June 1962. Judging by the external state of one of its resident C Class 0-6-0's No 31480, there were not many cleaners still employed at the depot. Anyway, time was not on the side of this engine with condemnation on the horizon. Taken out of service from Bricklayers Arms in July 1961, 31480 was scrapped at Ashford the same month. (N. L. Browne)

101) 70A Nine Elms based BR Class 5 4-6-0 No 73046 restarts its train and passes the raised inner home signal at Salisbury on
23rd July 1964. 73046 is devoid of front numberplate and is in an extremely sorry external state. It is not surprising that it
was withdrawn two months later. Despite the early demise of this engine, in September 1964, Salisbury was to remain a
bastion for Southern steam right up until the end in July 1967. (N. E. Preedy)

102) Newly transferred to 70D Eastleigh from 70E Salisbury, rebuilt *West Country* Class 4-6-2 No 34036 *Westward Ho* approaches the camera at Sway, between Southampton and Bournemouth with an unidentified express in September 1964. Constructed in July 1946, *Westward Ho* had been rebuilt during September 1960. It only helped to prolong its life until July 1967, being withdrawn from 70A Nine Elms. (G. W. Sharpe)

103) In pristine, ex. works condition, U Class 2-6-0 No 31634, from 70A Nine Elms, is travelling tender-first with a lengthy rake of empty coaching stock from Waterloo, seen here passing beneath the elevated signalbox at Clapham Junction in August 1955. Like *Westward Ho*, in the above picture, it also was withdrawn from Nine Elms, in the case of 31634, in December 1963. (N. L. Browne)

104) Never one to pass up a useful opportunity, the Running Shift Foreman at 75A Brighton has commandered L1 Class 4-4-0 No 31784, from 73B Bricklayers Arms for use on the 11.35am Brighton to Lancing goods. After working tender-first from Brighton Top Yard to Preston Park, the engine is now the right way round as it descends the Cliftonville spur to Hove and the West Coast line, on 26th August 1958. (Peter Hay)

105) Recently outshopped from Eastleigh Works, *Lord Nelson* Class 4-6-0 No 30852 *Sir Walter Raleigh* waits at Eastleigh to be returned to the local shed, coded 71A on 23rd May 1957. Behind 30852 is an unidentified S15 Class 4-6-0. *Sir Walter Raleigh* was to remain at Eastleigh shed until condemned in February 1962. It travelled under its own steam to Ashford Works for scrapping and was cut up the following month. (A. N. H. Glover)

106) A less than crowded shed scene at 70F Bournemouth on 14th August 1966. In steam outside the entrance to the depot is BR Class 5 4-6-0 No 73088 *Joyous Gard* (70C Guildford), the name of which was once allocated to *King Arthur* Class 4-6-0 No 30741, and rebuilt *West Country* Class 4-6-2 No 34047 *Callington* (rebuilt in November 1958), a local engine. Behind 73088 is BR Class 4 4-6-0 No 75065, a 70D Eastleigh engine. (T. R. Amos)

107) Special traffic at Eythorne on 19th May 1957. The passengers have just disembarked from this S.L.S. sponsored 'London, Chatham & Dover' train which was being hauled by 01 Class 0-6-0 No 31425, from 74C Dover. 31425 had been built by Sharp-Stewart in 1897 and rebuilt by Wainwright in 1914. Eythorne station, once owned by the East Kent Railway, had been closed since 1948. (F. Hornby)

108) Steam trains from the Oxted and East Grinstead lines only visited London Bridge during the rush hours and in March 1957 the crew of K Class 2-6-0 No 32346 (75E Three Bridges) take it easy after bringing in a load of City workers up to 'Town'. The train has terminated in the former SECR Low Level station and appropriately the leading vehicle is an SECR 'Birdcage' brake, No S3333S of 1909 vintage. (Peter Hay)

109) Grove Park, between Hither Green and Chislehurst, is the setting for this photograph of unrebuilt *Battle of Britain* Class 4-6-2 No 34084 *253 Squadron*, from 74B Ramsgate, as it passes the camera, light engine, on 28th September 1957. Built at Brighton Works by B.R. in 1948 *253 Squadron* was surplus to the Kent Coast motive power requirements in October 1960 and was drafted away to 72A Exmouth Junction. (F. Hornby)

110) In the 1980's, the area in and around Fawley is dominated by the massive oil refinery which can be seen from miles around. On 12th May 1956 there are only two large chimney's to be seen in the background as M7 Class 0-4-4T No 30378 (71A Eastleigh) makes ready to depart from the station with the 5.16pm local to Eastleigh. Fawley station, of LSWR origin, closed to passenger traffic in 1966. (F. Hornby)

111) The fireman of H Class 0-4-4T No 31512, a local engine, takes it easy at Faversham on a sunny 21st March 1959. Observing the huge lumps of coal which are present in the bunker of his charge, he will be able to dispense with his shovel and throw the coal in with his bare hands. Wagons, a buffer-stop, colour and dummy semaphore signals help to complete this picture. (N. L. Browne)

112) The almost deserted scene at 70A Nine Elms is dominated by the massive coaling plant on a May day in 1964. Obviously fresh from works, in front of the depot was a locally based rebuilt *Merchant Navy* Class 4-6-2 No 35026 *Lamport & Holt Line* which had been born in December 1948 and modified in January 1957. In September 1964, *Lamport & Holt Line* moved on to 70G Weymouth. (A. C. Ingram)

113) In the Spring of 1957, Templecombe still belonged to the Southern Region, a right it was to surrender to the Western Region in February 1958. BR Class 4 4-6-0 No 75073, from 71G Bath Green Park backs its three coach passenger stock into the sidings. When this duty was finished it would probably make for the local shed, coded 71H, for servicing. When taken over, Templecombe shed adopted the new code of 82G. (A. C. Ingram)

114) N Class 2-6-0 No 31403, from the not too distant shed at 75A Brighton, is at the rear (or the front) of a freight train at Hove, in March 1963. As it is not sporting any lamps or discs of any kind it is difficult to establish whether or not it is pulling or pushing the wagons. 31403 was in the twilight of its life, being condemned three short months after this picture was taken. (G. W. Sharpe)

115) Most prominent in this congested scene at 73D Gillingham, is push and pull fitted H Class 0-4-4T No 31308, a local engine, which was used for services to Allhallows on the Isle of Grain. Also on shed is N Class 2-6-0 31867, from 75B Redhill and unidentified members of Classes E1 4-4-0 (left) and C 0-6-0 alongside the shed wall, in September 1958. Gillingham lost its parent code in June 1959 and closed in June of the following year. (Peter Hay)

116) Another view of O2 Class 0-4-4T No 17 *Seaview* (70H Ryde), this time in action at Newport on the Isle of Wight on 7th August 1960. Built at Nine Elms in December 1891, *Seaview* was withdrawn exactly seventy-five years later, in December 1966. Newport had a shed of its own up until November 1957, coded 70G. Upon closure its allocation moved on to Ryde. (F. Hornby)

117) A cross view of the shed and part of the yard at 75F Tunbridge Wells on 5th September 1960. On view are four locomotives, three of which are BR Class 4 2-6-4 Tanks, one being identified as No 80142, a native of 75F. To the right of 80142, is E4 Class 0-6-2T No 32581, another local engine. Tunbridge became a sub-shed of Brighton in September 1963, then a sub of Redhill in June 1964 and closed in June 1965. (R. Picton)

118) Bright sunshine highlights the gleaming external appearance of *Schools* Class 4-4-0 No 30910 *Merchant Taylors* as it graces the yard, in steam, at Newhaven on 13th April 1958. *Merchant Taylors* was a 74B Ramsgate engine at this date in time but it was transferred to Nine Elms in June 1959 when Ramsgate lost its allocation. It only had a limited life at Nine Elms, being made redundant on a permanent basis in November 1961. (F. Hornby)

119) Unrebuilt *West Country* Class 4-6-2 No 34095 *Brentor*, from 70A Nine Elms, is traversing quadrupled track as it storms towards the camera at Worting Junction, in charge of an unidentified express – circa 1956. This was another of the British Railways built light Pacifics, being constructed in October 1949. Rebuilding came in January 1961 and withdrawal followed some six years later, in July 1967, from 70D Eastleigh. (G. W. Sharpe)

120) Sunlight and shadow in the yard at 70D Eastleigh on 5th February 1967. In the foreground is a soot-stained water column and a rusting brazier. The shadow of the water column and hose is being cast over a Bulleid Pacific, but not for much longer with the end of steam on the Southern only a few short months away. Being this late in the day, it was somewhat surprising that rebuilt *West Country* Class 4-6-2 No 34104 *Bere Alston*, a resident of Eastleigh since November 1961, still had its nameplate in situ. *Bere Alston* had a working life of seventeen years being built in April 1950, rebuilt during May 1961 and condemned in June 1967. (R. W. Hinton)

121) 73C Hither Green based, N1 Class 2-6-0 No 31879 drifts into Dartford station with a passenger train consisting of a mixed bag of stock, on 1st July 1957. To the right of the locomotive is one of the once common loading gauges. In this particular case it looks like a converted gallows. The N1 Class consisted of only six engines and all were withdrawn between October and November 1962. (John Smith)

122) BR Class 2 2-6-2T No 84022 (73B Bricklayers Arms) banks the down *Golden Arrow* up to Grosvenor Bridge, out of Victoria (Eastern Section) on 31st March 1961. Note the logo of a bicycle as applied to the rear of the enclosed goods van. The last batch of these engines, Nos 84020-84029 were allocated to the Southern Region between March and June 1957 but their lives were shortlived, the last ones being withdrawn in 1965. (F. Hornby)

123) Torrington station, in North Devon, is all but deserted in October 1962. Ex. LMR Ivatt Class 2 2-6-2T No 41312, from 72E Barnstaple Junction, is in charge of a one coach Barnstaple passenger working. The line was soon to be another victim of Dr. Beeching, with all of the intermediate stations between Barnstaple Junction and Halwill Junction closing in 1965 with the exception of Yarde Halt, closed in 1964. (R. C. Carpenter)

124) Although running a system dedicated to passenger electrification, the Southern Railway built modern concrete coaling plants at busy sheds like 74B Ramsgate. New arms for old water cranes were needed when Bulleid Pacifics with high tenders appeared on the scene. Was C Class 0-6-0 No 31271 reflecting on these changes as it stood in the sunshine after being serviced in April 1952? (Peter Hay)

125) Ex. GWR locomotives were a common sight at 75B Redhill, for they shared the services to and from Reading with Southern and BR Standard engines. The main Western types to be seen were from the 4300 Class 2-6-0's and *Manor* Class 4-6-0's. One of 81D Reading's 4300 Class 2-6-0's No 6302 is in steam in the yard at Redhill on 12th January 1957. (N. L. Browne)

126) The old Somerset & Dorset, or 'Slow and Dirty', main line was very much in use during the summer months, and double-heading of heavy holiday expresses was commonplace over this tortuous route. Ex. LMS Class 2P 4-4-0 No 40569 (71H Templecombe) and BR Class 5 4-6-0 No 73067 (16A Nottingham) combine to power the 9.25am Nottingham to Bournemouth train, near to Masbury on 4th September 1957. (J. Head)

127) A spruced up Wainwright H Class 0-4-4T No 31239 is ready for the road, with safety valves popping, in the yard of its home shed at 74D Tonbridge on 9th March 1957. One can almost hear the unique 'Ker-Chunk - Ker-Chunk' noises which were associated with the pump attached to the smokebox of these and other engines. 31239 survived at Tonbridge until condemned in January 1960. (N. L. Browne)

128) The driver and fireman of BR Class 4 2-6-0 No 76008 (72B Salisbury) chat to a group of young spotters gathered at the end of one of the platforms at Eastleigh on 1st August 1962. 76008 had not long arrived from Salisbury and with the discs re-arranged to show that it was now in charge of empty stock, it is waiting for a path which will take it to the close at hand carriage sidings. (N. L. Browne)

129) U Class 2-6-0 No 31639 (70C Guildford) trundles out of a siding at Cheam and sets off for Epsom with a short freight on a gloomy August day in 1963. In the foreground a Southern Railway notice states: DANGER – DON'T TOUCH CONDUCTOR RAILS, somewhat of an understatement. They should have clarified it with something like: IF YOU DO, THERE WILL BE A PUFF OF SMOKE AND IT WILL BE 'GOODNIGHT VIENNA'. (A. C. Ingram)

130) Bright sunshine reflects off the clean lines of N Class 2-6-0 No 31834, a resident of the shed at 72A Exmouth Junction on 9th July 1956. Exmouth Junction had a large number of these engines on its books for use over the Southern lines all over Devon. 31834, built at Ashford Works in 1924 remained in service at Exmouth until withdrawn in September 1964. Behind 31834 is unrebuilt *West Country* Class 4-6-2 No 34014 *Budleigh Salterton*. (F. Hornby)

131) The E6 Class was the last of the 'Billington Radials' (LBSCR 0-6-2T) to be designed and remained virtually unaltered in appearance till they were scrapped. In February 1957, No 32408 (73B Bricklayers Arms) was still very actively employed, working heavy coal trains over the steeply graded Deptford Wharf branch in South London. Notice the distinctive chimney and the pop safety valves set crosswise on the boiler. (Peter Hay)

132) On a bitterly cold but very bright 21st February 1960, USA Class 0-6-0T No 30065 is engaged on shunting duties between the 'New and Old' docks in Southampton. At this date in time, all fourteen members of the class were allocated to 71I Southampton Docks for use on similar duties. Withdrawn as DS237 in May 1967, 30065 is now preserved on the Keighley & Worth Valley Railway. (T. R. Amos)

133) Ex. SECR C Class 0-6-0 No 31112 stands on a centre road at Gravesend Central with empty coaching stock on 2nd August 1954. A member of the footplate staff is taking it easy, with his feet up, reading a newspaper. Based at 73D Gillingham, 31112 moved on to 70A Nine Elms in June 1959. Before withdrawal in April 1962 it also had spells at Dover and Ashford. (F. Hornby)

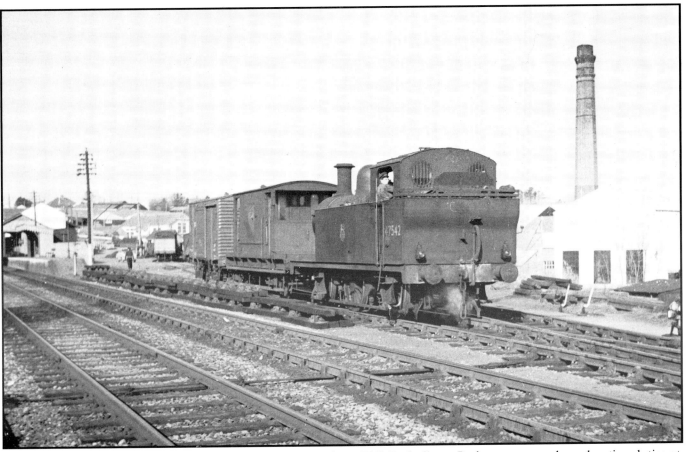

134) Ex. LMS Fowler 'Jinty' Class 3F 0-6-0T No 47542, from 71G Bath Green Park, was engaged on shunting duties at Sturminster Newton, between Templecombe and Blandford Forum in March 1957. In common with most of the ex. Somerset & Dorset stations and lines, Sturminster Newton closed completely in 1966. 47542 had been withdrawn some four years ealier, in June 1962, from Templecombe shed. (A. C. Ingram)

135) With Corfe Castle in the background, BR Class 4 2-6-4T No 80146, from 70F Bournemouth, passes through the delightful Dorset countryside with a three coach local passenger train from Wareham to Swanage on 8th August 1966. This branch line, with its only intermediate station at Corfe Castle, closed in 1972 but much of it has since been taken over by the preservationists. (T. R. Amos)

136) The clean condition of these three engines, on shed at 75A Brighton, gives the lie to stories that by 1955 engine cleaning was a thing of the past. E4 Class 0-6-2T No 32484 has buffered up to BR Class 4 2-6-4T No 80025, whilst in the background, is the distinctive firebox of a Brighton 'Atlantic', H2 Class 4-4-2 No 32421 *South Foreland*. (Peter Hay)

137) 73C Hither Green shed, in South-East London, was one of the first major depots on the Southern Region to be fully dieselised, in October 1961, though facilities for visiting steam locomotives remained for some time afterwards. On 5th September 1959, the yard and shed was still full of steam and in the foreground was one of its stud of C Class 0-6-0's No 31298, built at Ashford in 1908. (F. Hornby)

138) Orpington in Kent, between Petts Wood and Knockholt, is the setting for this mid-1949 print of C Class 0-6-0 No 31486, seen light engine in the station. Although it had been in British Railways ownership for some eighteen months, the logo of its old masters was still to be seen on the tender. This was a common sight to be seen on engines from all regions for many a year after 1948. (N. L. Browne)

139) Cleaned to perfection, BR *Britannia* Class 4-6-2 No 70014 *Iron Duke* (73A Stewarts Lane) approaches Ashford with the down *Golden Arrow* on 29th April 1956. Like its counterpart, 70004 *William Shakespeare*, 70014 was also the pride of Stewarts Lane and they both shared the bulk of the *Golden Arrow* workings until they were transferred to the London Midland Region shed at 14B Kentish Town in June 1958. Before condemnation in December 1967, *Iron Duke* had spells at Trafford Park, Newton Heath, Neasden, Annesley, Willesden (twice), Llandudno Junction (twice), Crewe (North), Crewe (South) – twice and Carlisle (Kingmoor) (J. Head)

140) With electric trains either side and the bastion of democracy, the Houses of Parliament, in the background, rebuilt *Merchant Navy* Class 4-6-2 No 35030 *Elder-Dempster Lines*, based at 70A Nine Elms, in superb external condition, threads its way through a maze of tracks on a perfect summer's day on 23rd July 1960. *Elder-Dempster Lines*, rebuilt in April 1958 is passing through Vauxhall with the down *Bournemouth Belle*. (N. L. Browne)

141) BR Class 4 4-6-0 No 75070, from 70A Nine Elms, is being employed on an RCTS sponsored special, seen here at Fareham, in the mid-sixties. As was the norm for locomotives being supplied for such duties, 75070 is in fine external fettle, but is minus its shedplate. Note that the disc showing the code SPL 2 on the smokebox door, has been hung upside-down. (G. W. Sharpe)

142) L1 Class 4-4-0 No 31789, a visitor from 74C Dover, in light steam, sizzles and gurgles on a side road at 75A Brighton on 12th January 1957. This particular locomotive was the final engine in the class, numerically speaking. Like its sister engines it was transferred to 70A Nine Elms in June 1959, being withdrawn from there in November 1961. (N. L. Browne)

143) Basingstoke station on 14th May 1955. *King Arthur* Class 4-6-0 No 30787 *Sir Menadeuke* (allocation not known), in magnificent condition, waits for the road to Waterloo with an up express. It was more than likely a 71A Eastleigh engine, being withdrawn from there in February 1959. As a point of interest, in January 1957, eleven Arthur's were based at Eastleigh, these being Nos 30748/63/70/84-91. (F. Hornby)

144) Ex. LMS Ivatt Class 2 2-6-2T No 41308 (72A Exmouth Junction), departs from Axminster with its one coach branch train to Lyme Regis on 22nd April 1963. This line and the two stations associated with it, at Combpyne and Lyme Regis closed in 1965. In the distance, to the right of 41308, on a goods train, is unrebuilt *West Country* Class 4-6-2 No 34015 *Exmouth*, also from Exmouth Junction shed. (B. W. L. Brooksbank)

145) The driver and fireman look forward from the cab of their charge, ex. SECR R1 Class 0-6-0T No 31337 (74C Dover), which has steam to spare whilst awaiting its next duty at Folkestone Junction. These locomotives were often employed on pilot or banking jobs with heavy boat trains from Folkestone Harbour and they were kept in the small shed at the Junction, overnight. (F. Hornby)

146) The engines which brought in the empty stock of boat trains were often required to bank the outgoing service out of the platforms at Victoria, to help the train get a run at the 1 in 64 bank up to Grosvenor Bridge. In June 1957, H Class 0-4-4T No 31261, from 73A Stewarts Lane, is doing its bit for the departing 'Ostend Boat Express'. (Peter Hay)

147) The Lyme Regis branch, though a creation of this century, had all the things a country branch should have. Here at Lyme on 1st August 1959 we can see the tiny wooden signalbox and on the right the diminutive engine shed. Quite properly, the engines were survivors, not to be found elsewhere: the Adams 4-4-2T of Class 0415. No 30583 (72A Exmouth Junction) dated from 1885 is happily still with us on the Bluebell Railway. (Peter Hay)

148) The Southern Railway Class Q 0-6-0's originally had Maunsell's lipped chimney, then later the wide Bulleid variety. No 30545 finished its career with the BR Class 4 type. 30545, based at 75E Three Bridges, heads a freight train near to Wivelsfield on the Brighton line in May 1960. This engine was drafted to 70A Nine Elms in January 1964, ending its days there in April 1965. (Peter Hay)

149) Unrebuilt *Merchant Navy* Class 4-6-2 No 35014 *Nederland Line* (70A Nine Elms) speeds the up *Royal Wessex*, bound for Waterloo, through Surbiton on the outskirts of London on 14th May 1955. All of the stock of the *Royal Wessex* was of the 'blood and custard' variety. Built during February 1945, *Nederland Line* was modified in July 1956. It was transferred from Nine Elms to 70G Weymouth in September 1964 and withdrawn from there in March 1967. (F. Hornby)

150) This picture shows that the structures on the East Grinstead - Lewes line were built to accommodate double track but the anticipated volume of traffic never came about and by June 1954 many of the trains ran almost empty. C2X Class 0-6-0 No 32536 is at the head of the 2.59pm from East Grinstead, seen here leaving Barcombe. This station closed the following year. (Peter Hay)

151) Despite the Maunsell chimney and smokebox, the drop in the footplating and a high arched cab roof identifies S15 Class 4-6-0 No 30509 as one of the LSWR built first series of the class. On 8th July 1957, 30509 had arrived at 70F Fratton shed, in Portsmouth, on a goods working from 70B Feltham, home of so many of its type. Withdrawn from there in July 1963, 30509 was disposed of at Cohens, Kettering in March 1964. (Peter Hay)

152) Steam blows from the safety valves of rebuilt *West Country* Class 4-6-2 No 34022 *Exmoor* (70D Eastleigh) as it is serviced alongside Basingstoke shed on 29th August 1964. In front of *Exmoor*, rebuilt in December 1957, is ex. GWR *Grange* Class 4-6-0 No 6878 *Longford Grange*, from 85A Worcester, minus nameplates. Basingstoke, once coded 70D had lost its allocation in March 1963 becoming a sub-shed of Eastleigh. (C. Stacey)

153) The country pick-up goods is now a thing of the past but on 1st June 1957 it was still a common sight. A look at the load behind C Class 0-6-0 No 31272, from 74D Tonbridge, at Horam in Sussex shows why it was uneconomic. Horam, or to give it its full title of Waldron and Horam Road on the Eridge to Polegate line, closed in 1965. (Peter Hay)

154) The C2X Class 0-6-0's were strange and ungainly looking machines with their extended smokeboxes and double domes astride the boiler. They were Marsh rebuilds of the original Billington designed C2 Class, introduced in 1908. No 32527 was one of a number of these engines which were based at 75E Three Bridges. It is seen here in the home depot yard on 25th May 1957. (A. N. H. Glover)

155) An unkempt rebuilt *Merchant Navy* Class 4-6-2 No 35028 *Clan Line* (70A Nine Elms) speeds through Raynes Park, between New Malden and Wimbledon, almost at the end of its journey from Bournemouth, with the up *Bournemouth Belle* on 18th May 1964. Built by BR in December 1948, *Clan Line* was later rebuilt at Eastleigh in October 1959. Withdrawn from Nine Elms in July 1967 it was saved for posterity by the M.N.L.P.S. (B. W. L. Brooksbank)

156) Another rebuilt *Merchant Navy* Class 4-6-2 in action, this time in the shape of No 35024 *East Asiatic Company*, also from 70A Nine Elms, as it storms through Seaton Junction at the head of the down 'A.C.E.' – *Atlantic Coast Express* on 14th April 1962. Like 35028, *East Asiatic Company* was a product of the B.R. workshops, in November 1948. Modified to its final condition in October 1959 it was condemned in January 1965 from 70G Weymouth. (R. Picton)

157) The M7 Class 0-4-4 Tank locomotives were of a compact and handsome design, as can be seen of this close-up photograph of No 30125 in the yard of its home shed at 71A Eastleigh in July 1951. Its latter years of service were from 72A Exmouth Junction, where it had been since October 1960. After withdrawal from there in December 1962 it was stored for over twelve months at Exmouth and Eastleigh before being cut up in February 1964. (G. W. Sharpe)

158) The second Bulleid Pacific to be constructed, in June 1945, was never rebuilt, therefore it never lost its air-smoothed casing throughout its twenty-two year working life. In this picture *West Country* Class 4-6-2 No 34002 *Salisbury*, from 70A Nine Elms, accelerates a Waterloo - Bournemouth express through Basingstoke, over newly laid third rail tracks, which were to be the death knell of Southern steam, on 11th June 1966. Despite being rather grubby in appearance, *Salisbury* still retained the number and nameplates. Condemned in April 1967, 34002 was scrapped at Cashmores, Newport around October 1967. (N. E. Preedy)

159) Almost at the end of its lengthy career, H Class 0-4-4T No 31543, from 75F Tunbridge Wells, arrives at Oxted with its two coach vintage set in May 1963. At this stage in time there were only seven of these locomotives still in service, these being Nos 31005, 31263, 31518, 31522, 31543, 31544 and 31551, all based at Tunbridge Wells. The last survivors, Nos 31263, 31518 and 31551, were all withdrawn in January 1964. (G. W. Sharpe)

160) A filthy dirty BR Class 4 2-6-0 No 76025, a 71A Eastleigh engine, passes Worting Junction, near Basingstoke, with the 9.05am Sheffield (Victoria) to Bournemouth express on 16th July 1960. The authorities must have been short of motive power on this day, having to press a Class 4 engine into service with this fairly heavy express, which was probably running rather late. (B. W. L. Brooksbank)

161) The summer of 1964 still saw a large amount of steam workings on heavy express duties to and from Waterloo to Exeter. On 18th May 1964 one of the 70A Nine Elms stud of rebuilt *Merchant Navy* Class 4-6-2's No 35012 *United States Line*, built in December 1944 and rebuilt in February 1957, climbs up Honiton Bank in the West Country with a heavily loaded passenger working. (R. Picton)

162) Three generations of Western Section motive power are visible in this line-up at 70A Nine Elms on 22nd March 1957. Urie is represented by the distinctive smokebox of a rebuilt 700 Class 0-6-0, on the left, and two Bulleid Pacifics – one of them being unrebuilt *Merchant Navy* Class 4-6-2 No 35021 *New Zealand Line* – are obscured by a Drummond M7 Class 0-4-4T No 30319, a resident of Nine Elms. (Peter Hay)

163) A photograph of Ryde shed building from an unusual angle, on 19th September 1964. Compared to most steam sheds, it looked nothing like one, more like a small factory on an industrial estate. Originally the property of the Isle of Wight Railway, it was taken over by the Southern and later by British Railways in 1948. It was coded 71F from 1950-54 and then 70H until closure in March 1967. (R. Picton)

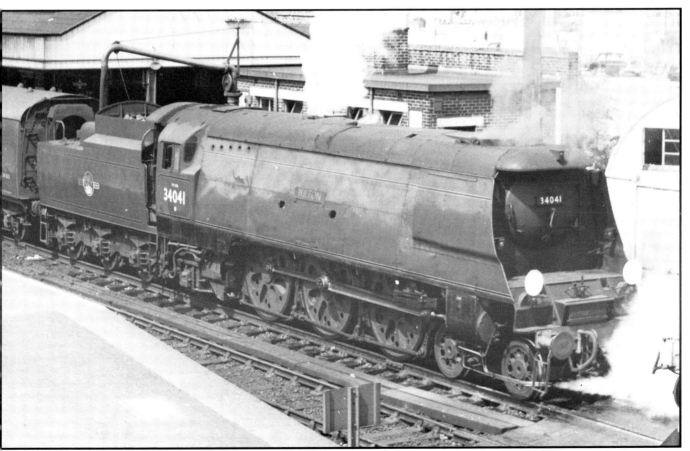

164) Unrebuilt *West Country* Class 4-6-2 No 34041 *Wilton* (71B Bournemouth), primed and ready for the road, is taking refreshment at Southampton (Central) in the summer of 1962. *Wilton*, constructed in September 1946 was in charge of a Bournemouth - Waterloo express. Condemned from 70D Eastleigh in January 1966, 34041 was despatched to South Wales for scrapping, being cut up at Cashmores, Newport around May 1966. (G. W. Sharpe)

165) The handsome design of the *Schools* Class 4-4-0's is clear to be seen in this photograph of No 30925 *Cheltenham*, at rest outside its home shed of 73B Bricklayers Arms, in company with an unidentified sister engine on 5th March 1960. Withdrawn from 70D Basingstoke in December 1962, *Cheltenham* was stored at various B.R. depots for many years. Now it is a working member of the National Railway Museum, York. (N. L. Browne)

166) One of the celebrated 0298 Class Beattie Well Tanks trundles out of woodland, on one of its regular duties which it had been on for so many years, the Wenford Bridge china clay branch near Wadebridge. No 30587 (72F Wadebridge) is approaching Dunmere Crossing on its return from Wenford Bridge, in July 1958. The shed in which it was housed, closed in November 1964. (Peter Hay)

167) M7 Class 0-4-4T No 30049, from 75D Horsham, simmers at the head of its two coach push and pull train, in Guildford station, in August 1952. Horsham shed, was rather unusual in design, consisting of a half-roundhouse with the turntable in the open, as indeed was the shed at Guildford. It became a sub-shed of 75E Three Bridges in June 1959, then of 75A Brighton in January 1964 and closed in June of the same year. (G. W. Sharpe)

168) C Class 0-6-0 No 31510 stands amidst various discarded bric a brac, in front of the shed building at 73D Gillingham where it lived on 21st March 1959. Moving on to 70A Nine Elms in June 1959, 31510 found itself on the move once more in October 1961, this time to 73B Bricklayers Arms. A final transfer in June 1962 to 75D Stewarts Lane saw it condemned the same month. (N. L. Browne)

169) It was very rare to see any of the Bulleid Pacifics on freight duties but in March 1965 rebuilt *West Country* Class 4-6-2 No 34039 *Boscastle* (70D Eastleigh) was seconded to such a task, probably because withdrawal was only two months away, and it was seen here leaving the sidings at Fleet. Vintage of September 1946 and rebuilt in October 1960, *Boscastle* is now in safe hands at Loughborough. (G. W. Sharpe)

170) All seventeen members of the K Class 2-6-0's were condemned in November and December 1962 from Brighton and Three Bridges depots. They were dumped as and where they were given the order to douse their fires for the last time, most at their former home sheds, whilst others were already at Eastleigh Works. Still stored at 75E Three Bridges on 21st April 1963 was No 32353. It was eventually cut up at Eastleigh in December 1963. (T. R. Amos)

71) Another close-up photograph of the popular Drummond M7 Class 0-4-4 Tanks. This example, No 30128 (shed unknown) is captured by the camera, in steam, in the shed yard at 71A Eastleigh on 2nd June 1951. In the latter years, from January 1957 at least, it was based at 71B Bournemouth from whence it was withdrawn in January 1961 and cut up the following month. (A. N. H. Glover)

72) Ex. LMS Ivatt Class 2 2-6-2T No 41313, with a friendly driver looking from the cab, is in company with an unidentified M7 Class 0-4-4T at Barnstaple Junction station on 29th June 1960. 41313 allocated to the local shed of 72E, moved on to 75A Brighton in March 1963. Like so many engines of its type it ended up on the South Western section, at 70D Eastleigh in May 1964 and was condemned in November 1965. (N. L. Browne)

173) High pressure steam bursts from the safety valves of unrebuilt *West Country* Class 4-6-2 No 34092 *City of Wells* (73A Stewarts Lane) as it approaches Maidstone with an August Bank Holiday special in 1959. The twelve coaches of this formation are a real mixed bag of stock. Built in September 1949 by B.R., *City of Wells* was taken out of service in November 1964 and is now the pride of the Keighley & Worth Valley Railway. (Brian Coates)

174) In steam days Redhill was a place not only where trains changed engines but also where engine crews were relieved. This is taking place as H Class 0-4-4T No 31259 stands on the down through line in the weak winter sun of February 1952. Condemned from 73J Tonbridge in November 1959, 31259 spent a brief period of storage at Ashford Works before being scrapped in January 1960. (Peter Hay)

175) Salisbury was a meeting place for both Southern and Western Region engines. Spotters of all ages witness the impending departure of ex. GWR *Hall* Class 4-6-0 No 6917 *Oldlands Hall*, from 84B Oxley (Wolverhampton) which is in charge of a cross-country express V08 on 27th July 1963. Next to *Oldlands Hall* is rebuilt *West Country* Class 4-6-2 No 34017 *Ilfracombe* (rebuilt November 1957), from Nine Elms. (B. W. L. Brooksbank)

176) The confusion of equipment beside the smokebox of M7 Class 0-4-4T No 30047 (75D Horsham) is for the compressed air equipment for train control when pushing instead of pulling, the van next to the engine being specially piped so that it could run in these 'motor train' workings. On 13th October 1957, the 2.19pm from Horsham to Brighton is slowing for its call at Henfield, which was to close in 1966. (Peter Hay)

177) We started this album rolling with a photograph of unrebuilt *Merchant Navy* Class 4-6-2 No 35021 *New Zealand Line*, from 71B Bournemouth, at Waterloo in April 1959. We catch a last glimpse of her, with well oiled motion, resting within the confines of the running shed at 71A Eastleigh on 26th April 1958. *New Zealand Line* was the first *Merchant Navy* to be built by B.R., in September 1948 and was withdrawn in August 1965. (F. Hornby)

178) We also end where we began, at Waterloo station, on a June day in 1964. Although BR Class 5 4-6-0 No 73113 *Lyonnesse*, in quite atrocious external condition, from 70A Nine Elms, is displaying a Waterloo - Bournemouth headcode, it was performing on station pilot duties. The name *Lyonnesse* as applied to 73113 was once carried by *King Arthur* Class 4-6-0 No 30743. (Brian Coates)